Parallel Lines

Parallel Lines

Pam Galloway

Ekstasis Editions

Library and Archives Canada Cataloguing in Publication

Galloway, Pam
   Parallel lines / Pam Galloway.

   Poems.

ISBN 1-894800-71-0

   I. Title.

PS8613.A4597P37 2006   C811'.6   C2006-906621-0

© 2006 Pam Galloway
Cover art:

Published in 2006 by:
Ekstasis Editions Canada Ltd.   Ekstasis Editions
Box 8474, Main Postal Outlet   Box 571
Victoria, B.C. V8W 3S1   Banff, Alberta ToL oCo

Parallel Lines has been published with the assistance of grants from the Canada Council for the Arts and the British Columbia Arts Council administered by the Cultural Services Branch of the Government of British Columbia. .

*For my parents: Lilian, who taught me to love poetry
and Gordon, who showed me the way back in time.*

Contents

Number 17 Aqueduct Street

Still Life	15
Wise Woman	16
The Local Woman Who 'Did'	18
Water Ways	19
Jack Brady's Canal	21
Searching	22
It's the Voices	24
My Family Addresses a Glass of Stout	25
Army Form B. 104_82A	27
How to Imagine Your Father	29
18 Holt Street	30

A Crevasse Too Wide

Smaller Than a Distant Star	33
Bloom—May 1953	34
Scatter the Good Seed	35
The Wrong Kind of Cry	37
Sun-Rays	39
Distant Voices	40
Church Militant	41
Whit Walks (at Pentecost)	42
Break	43
Skies	44

A Northern Album

Purden Lake	47
The Artist's Wife	48
November Lights	49
Hihium Colours	50
Hihium—Home	51`
Captured	52
Genesis	53
Traces	54
The Comfort of Rain	
Circle	55
Woman's Tongue Leaf	56
Imagine	58
Dear Ann	59
In Silhouette	60
Farewell	61

What We Keep

Beside an Ocean, Under a Sky	65
Nitobe—Reflections	67
Nitobe—Water Lily	68
Reflection	69
Ocean in a Room	70
Temperate	71
Silent Film	72
Always, Two Voices	73
What Enters	74
Ocean Bed	75
Some Days	76
What We Keep	77
Eevy, Ivy, Over	78
Into the Light	80
The Promise	82
Harbinger	83
Correspondence	84

Parallel Lines

Parallel lines

You will see this country before me.
I flew to its furthest coast, settled
behind a wall of mountains, looked out
across islands that point west, my back to you
and the continent between us.

I have imagined Ontario, the land unfolding,
hills in the distance, maple forests
turning the horizon red. And the prairies:
one immense golden belly sunning itself
under a huge sky.

Not intimidated by its girth, you have decided
to journey across Canada's stretched skin,
your questions of geography and history
only dimples in the surface.

I will see it when I'm ready to turn
and when I'm ready to leave this rocky shelf,
the home I've stolen from the forest,
walls of hemlock, windows of rain.

I imagine you leaning from the train window
looking far into the distance
where the rail tracks converge, looking forward
to the end of your journey, where we will come together.
You are thinking about parallel lines.
How they create an illusion.
How they hold each other apart.

Number 17 Aqueduct Street

Still Life

Straight-backed chair at a front-door step.
Wood's bone-pale scratches, concrete's
solid grey. Place a woman there. Stand her
at the threshold, one hand steady on the frame,
about to step out, your grandma at the doorstep.

My finger on the photo's edge— mottled orange glue
has roughened the paper's gloss. I try
to find texture of Granny, through
flat greys: her hair gathered in a net, her face,
with resolute creases, her garden of an apron;
I feel for the spot to let me in beside her,
to crouch on the step
and watch

as she calls the neighbours over, stops the bookie
for the racing form, places her daily bet,
all of it—in silence. Children
whip noiseless hoops across cobbles, rag-man's dray
lifts hooves that never land.

Wise Woman

Annie

but her name was Hannah.
You found her birth certificate:
Father: John Brady — boatman. Mother:
Elizabeth Brady — her mark was a cross.
Always known as Annie, a good
northern name not fancy,
not posh.

She sang. A glass or two of sweet stout
smoothed down her song-dry throat,

I'll take you home again Kathleen

She leaned into the tune, glass in hand, marked
the falls and rises, holding it high at the pauses,
the other hand steadying
the piano-player's shoulder.

So what if she was a fighter? She'd say her piece on the street,
or in the pub — defend it with tucked-up skirts, lunged
and grabbed coat lapels, once: Jimmy Dupree's curly red mop.
Bundled and calmed in a fireman's lift
and delivered to her bed, Annie still had
Jimmy's tartan scarf, her trophy, draped round her neck.
Next day, upright and straightened out,
a newly pressed skirt, *Hannah*
stepped out to greet the milkman.

Thus did Hannah Brady marry Thomas Wise,
lived up to her new name.

The local woman, always there,
knowing what to do. Mid-wife one day,
she'd shut the eyes of the dead the next.

Eleven babies came, she raised seven.
They say she never wept.
Except the day the bookie died. Lace hanky clasped
to her bosom, she reached out, let darkness
take her grief, drew the parlour's velvet curtains
edge to edge. Refused to hear
your pleas on this,
your wedding day.
She closed the solid panelled door.
Sat alone.

The Local Woman Who 'Did'

Eh up, what's up now, what's up? she says
as Enid stares, one hand fast on the table-edge,
the other spread on her belly, her eyes
round and white as pickled eggs.
"How, Mrs Wise? It's coming – but how?
How will it get out?"

Same way it got in, lass,
just get a grip there.

And so it'll not be long now, for this young woman,
whose baby will come when and how he pleases.
She'll grip all right, grip sheets damp, crumpled,
but Annie will straighten them, smooth again for her to lie in,
knuckles shoved to her mouth, only a thin cry now, and squeezing,
pressing hard against the tight edge, the lip
her body's made to hold her baby in.
Poor Enid wanting out.

Bite down lass and— push, easy goes it, easy, now.

Annie's hands are ready, hold her thigh, *steady lass.*
Her shivering legs, those hands, her cries,
that *steady lass*, all slip together.
Here's an opening for that last and first effort.
Annie's hands wait to bring the child to the breast,
his mouth clamps down and quiet.
That's how, love, that's how.

Water Ways

A single drop,
tear-shaped cartoon glistening
with determination
for the start

One piece of paper,
a birth certificate,
set me looking.

One drop
into a deluge, fills a valley-bottom,
force and persistence in its route
to its single goal: the sea.

Your stories
were a slow-moving river.

Logs, rocks, entire trees
drag in the current, swirl under and over
white water, rest in dark pools until
water swells, rolls,
saunters, and diverted
from the river, finds its leveler:
the canal.
Released—gush of water
through a lock's scuppers—
the canal spills, re-fills and a boat
is lifted against a climb.

I allowed myself to float,
More voices filling my head:
her children, the neighbours,
the words swirling
as faces surfaced and sank back.

Passive shiftings carry loads of cotton,
coal, cloth in slow-motion.
Water sits, oily, grime-darkened,
marks the boat as it slides along
these narrow slots of water-ways.
Slow moves and the weighted vowels
of canal-side banter are built here,
solid as brick and stone and sheets
of steel-edged rain.

I found myself carried,
my ancestors loading me down:
photos from boxes, brittle tape
crumbling along gaping edges;
stories told in letters, recounted
over endless cups of tea; rumours,
gossip, truth—long-buried.

Jack Brady's Canal

I take your photo and you take mine under "Aqueduct St."
brightly signed on an office building's fresh red-bricked face.
Across the street could be a movie set: the nineteenth century
holding its own in one short, dilapidated row of tenements,
simple bricked-up boxes; wasteland all around: gravel and dirt
patched with unstoppable crabgrass, bramble,
the odd sunburst of dandelion.
Flagstones under our feet have cracked, sunk in places, lifted in others.
As we walk, we imagine your Granny once playing here,
her hopscotch scrawls patterning the pavement;
her father Jack's walk from work to home,
Annie skipping to meet him, down by the canal.

Where is the canal? Your hands, deep in your pockets, push
the thin fabric of your jacket straight, your lips a tense line.
Everything about you is set. You stare
past the office buildings. You're looking past car parks
sectioned off by chain-link fences but what you see
is Jack, rising early, striding out. *This way*—
and I run after you. We cross the road, detour round a factory,
shortcut through the car park, down a slope and there it is:
Jack's walk from number 17 to canal,
little more than a short horseshoe throw.

We walk the tow-path. Up-scale apartments range along both banks,
a flourish of Victorian wrought iron on their bland faces
reflects in the still and clean water. Mill and factory waste long-since dredged
and banks stripped of the suffocation of weeds, office workers walk here,
respect the new tone and carry their Starbucks' cups away,
back over the shiny-white, story-book bridge.
Everything's in order. A pristine, painted scrim
dropped over Jack Brady's time. All possibility of him lifted,
along with the mills' and warehouses' smog-blurred blackened walls.

Searching

Looking demands an object to be found.
It is the eyes' work. Or the hands
groping down the sides of sofas
pulling at pens, toys long lost and always
coins—some no longer legal tender.
There will be a shape, a form, something
to run a finger along, an edge to give it away.
How then to search out a voice?

Cosseted and regal, she lay in a high bed
the last years of her life. Sleeping, in my silent memory.
Her last breath blew a thin whistle, no words
anyone recalls; I wasn't there.

But Sundays, I used to arrive after Sunday school.
I stood beside her bed or crouched
on her *get-in-and-out* stool; I never saw her move.
Surely she was a queen, propped on pillows,
her fingers crooked the fold of the sheet,
her skin mottled as if she'd dipped
herself into vinegar—after years
of pickled cukes and onions, beetroots
and red cabbage, preserving herself
would have been a grand, *grand finale.*

I remember as I waited
and watched her for my allotted time:
my distraction, the soda syphon,
in its silver-topped opulence,
over at my house nothing so fancy—
not even close—milk bottles
and jugs of beer but, here, a soda syphon
glistered on its tray
beside the aspidistra
and I could have one glass.

I held one in my hand,
turned it to see the engraving of Blackpool Tower.
The cheap, shot glass as precious as the sparkling liquid
I'd squirt in. A delicate task: pressure on the trigger just right or nothing
would come or else too much, all over my Sunday best dress. I learned it,
then, the drinking: two mouthfuls and all gone
or, to sip, burst each bubble over my tongue;
these, not the empty taste of soda appealed.

She slept or watched me rearrange the glasses.
She must have said something but I cannot hold her up
to the ear of memory. I see her
sitting on a kitchen chair by the front door, watching
the street, shouting comments,
directing the action:
played out like an epic
from the filthy banks of the canal,
projected, an old, sepia-tinted silent flick
her voice slipped between the frames,
under the tinkle of soda, asleep.

It's The Voices

sounding down the stories.

Your memories the thread between us,
your mother's words ravelled from laughter
and her mother's, silent so long.

Annie's brogue like the best of the stew, I'll stir it,
thick, from the bottom of the pot.

Old words rolling like a boy's hoop thrashed with a stick
over cobblestones, spinning and clattering
as you chased it home.

Old words turning, with the stamp of brittle steps
across a lino floor, your parents dancing.

Old words lifting like your Granny's songs
Saturday nights in The Fox. Lift a glass,
sway in time, forget the houses row on row,
dark streets slick with another rain.
Repeat the chorus, make this 'Picardy,'
where voices bloom.

My Family Addresses a Glass of Stout

Weighing up the sleeve, the body
of ale stirring a pale efflorescence,
its bloom rising in slow motion
through the clearing dark,
Jack leans into the chair, cap back,
arms across his chest.
"Aye, it's reet enough," as he reaches out,
circles the base of the glass
with calloused fingers, smacks his lips.

Annie is sipping, each delicate draw
leaves a line of froth-blossom
along her lip, a measured tasting,
while she considers each an' a'
and her hand smoothes the table cloth,
it straightens us around the table.

"Eh, I'll not forget that day in May,
our Pamela." Nana, Lily, opens the door,
adds another empty to the line of dead bottles
growing on the step, takes in the fresh ones
her daughter's brought from the pub, the family waiting
for the latest, you with Lily
on guard, one room below my toiling mother
and I am ready to best foot the hot May day
to be celebrated in ice-cream and another glass of Mackeson.

You aren't drinking. Or speaking. Stare through
your glass to me: *the knack you have of doing things.*
Fancy getting them here, fancy
knowing where to look.
I winkled them out
of fusty parlours, funereal velour
and shining antimacassars;
gas lit streets, flickering
marriages, births and deaths;
lines on yellowed paper, the shivering edge.

Now I have them, I could whisper
in each ear: *tell us about the children whose names*
are ghosts; let us hear about Thomas, your loves,
your loss; speak of a child given up at birth,
of a husband drowned; tell her now
that you loved her but never said.
But my hands are under the table, fiddling
for the key that will let my family step
over the threshold, into
Number 17 Aqueduct Street.

Army Form B. 104_82A

(*in memory of Sapper Edmund Galloway 1905-1943*)

Madam, it is my painful duty to inform you...

full of pain
(a tooth throbbing deep
hot coals in a thimble)

or, the telegram shaking
in your hand and a hole gouged
huge and full of emptiness
in your chest.

...that no further news having been received...

no news used to be good, now means nothing
has happened, been reported,
been said. Seven months
of nothing, silence since the ship —
say nothing (if you can't
say something nice) — and look
the other way, look
at the soldiers and sailors
returning, touching
medals pinned in place.

...the Army Council have been regretfully constrained to conclude...

a matter of necessity
urged to do this, to come to this.
An unspoken
authority dared to think —

still would not say — now
breaks the silence
in disguise,
the official grey cloak.

27

...I am to express the sympathy and regret of the Army Council...

who are you who says this for them,
told to say this much
that they can't say, won't say
for themselves. They would want to,
understand this much, they are definitely
wanting

...the soldier's death in his Country's service...

he must have known it
was his, though he knew so little,
a few square miles of soot and smog-blackened brick,
a fragment of the country.
He stood up, he lived
he died.

No....C1/82A/2M
(If replying, please quote above No.)

How To Imagine Your Father

Did he fall, slide or somersault
into gaping grey, numbing
monochrome, the sea—
sudden vacuum—sucking the colours
from his eyes, the songs out of his lungs,
coming down around him like the last smog
to swallow a city?

How long did he know
what was coming, where in the ship—
the torpedo hit— where
did it throw him, what words did he shout
to his mates or them to him when they knew
the ship was sinking, how fast—what prayers,
what memories, what cries—

His words have washed in relentlessly.
The postcards: always *Look after your Mam,*
and the telegram: *Regret. Missing. Presumed.*
Dead, all these years and the sea
still turns.

18 Holt Street

Night came quick, the sky heavy
with cloud and factory smoke hanging
over the street like a damp sheet pegged out
and no wind.

Stair-rod rain slashed down
onto cobbles in need of a shining.
The rain at the windows, insistent tapping
forewarning of the knocker-up who'd come all too soon.

Nowhere to go and nowt to spend
you tuned in the wireless
up and down the tin-whistle wavelengths
and over the crackle came *Dick Barton, Special Agent.*

Another lump of coal on the fire—
posh as the next, you were—tile fireplace now.
Thin curtains drawn against the street's
softly buzzing gaslight glow.

Those four small rooms were yours at 8s 4d a week.
One cold tap at the brown pot sink, and a bath
made of tin, hung on a nail in the yard.
It was enough. A start.

Fifty years flicked by,
a playing-card waterfall: kids, telly, soon
a house with a garden. Remember
the record-player and *Moon River,* over and over?

There's no stopping the memories
stacking up at your feet. Pick one,
any one, hold it in your palm.
Let's have a look-see.

A Crevasse Too Wide

Smaller Than a Distant Star, August 1952

Heat presses down, between,
inside red-bricked houses
lining narrow streets and alleys.
Sticky tar-smell rises, lifts over the roof-top,
finds the patch of ambered sky.

Smaller than the stars, more distant
even than they are
and unimagined, I wait
between Gordon and Lilian who sit
out on the front step, his arm curled loosely
round her shoulders. They talk
across the street
to neighbours, their voices the only traffic.
Soon, they go in, shut the door behind me.
I follow as they move together,
find a room inside my mother.
There's not much space
to turn. I will grow
contained. Trace my fingers
along red walls.

That night, as she sleeps, she will
face the window and dream a place
of mountains and trees grown too tall and
land rolled flat and no end to it.

Bloom—May 1953

My mother ate ice cream while she laboured
on over-stuffed pillows.
Black and white striped ticking
shone through the pillowcases.
At ease in her own bed, she would have it her way.
Mid-July had arrived in May and no fridge in the house,
no soothing slivers of ice to be had,
she sent to the corner shop for ice-cream,
mound of smooth white
sweetness slipping into her mouth.

No modern birth this,
no belts strapped round her belly
feeding bleeps and scratches to a machine.
She held on to each contraction, felt the bud of her daughter
stirring in her womb,
tagged instructions for the mid-wife
to the end of each long-stemmed breath,
opened herself the way a flower unfolds in slow motion,
petal by precise petal.

Scatter the Good Seed

Today: piano.
The woman next door is practising.
I know the words.

We plough the fields and scatter
The good seed on the land.
And it is fed and watered
By God's almighty hand.

She's playing my childhood.
Her fingers tread the keys,
a stilted style to tease song
from the congregation.

Holy, holy, holy
Lord God almighty
Early in the morning
Our song will rise to thee.

> I stared into a wall of good winter coats,
> some of them I knew: Mr. Emmott from the shop
> was a dark blue mac. And Mrs E, in brown,
> big-bummed and woolly.
> The Ryans wore grey and black
> and Mrs Winter's red flashed a bit of colour
> into straight-laced Sunday. She wore scarlet lipstick too
> and always sang the wrong tune,
> but Mam said, "it's harmony" and "what a lovely voice"
> but I thought she was showing off.

They stood bolt upright for the vicar's inspection
hoping he'd not get the whiff of ale
that still blew from their lips after last night's pub-do.
Singing, but was God listening?

I looked for Him, up behind the dangling lights
beyond their glare, in the rafters' shadows.

The Reverand fired off words, spit-propelled bullets.
His eyes, red face, ordered me to *pay attention, lass.*
"What's up wi' him?" Mam yanked my arm.
"Stop fidgeting child!"
I stared ahead then found a hanky
in my pocket, and twisted it
round my finger, laced the edging into rings.
When he'd finished, there'd be tea and for my biscuit
I'd get a jammy dodger and dunk it soggy.

The Wrong Kind of Cry

We almost lost you

> and I imagined a forest, sky darkening,
> the three of us playing peek-a-boo
> behind trees
> a small girl running and running
> crouching inside ferns, listening
> to her parents call her name.

It wasn't that.

We almost lost you

I imagine
how you held
me, my skin burning, and you
not knowing—
my skin sticky, eyes
too bright and the crying,high
and thin and nothing
would stop it—and you not knowing
what to do. *What to do? Hush baby,*
> *hush*, rock her, swaddle her, sing lullabyes
> till the doctor comes.
> *Please, doctor, come.*

Handing you over was terrible

suddenly your arms were empty,
your sleeves still wet from holding me, my sweat
drying on the sheet you wrapped me in. Wan
hospital walls, bordered sickly green,
a row of cold straight-backed metal chairs, I picture you
waiting and pacing

I gave you my pain
too big for me to hold.

We weren't allowed to touch you

Needles and tubes threaded me
to life, a plastic tent around me—crystal air.
Streptomycin's success rates were magic chants
in your head as you watched every shallow breath.

We wondered if you'd ever wake.

Sun-Rays

Don't ever forget this:
ice-cold, clear jelly
slopped on my head; an urge to reach up,
slip my fingers into it slithering there. *Goo.*
Maybe it's alive, if it slips
a bit, it might drip down my face.

Nurses. A doctor. White coats, stiff aprons.
They attach wires to my head
and to a machine. Circular tingles on my scalp;
the machine burps a paper message, my brain speaking
in squiggles. I don't understand a word.

My hair and the jelly lie slimed on my head for hours
like trails of cold gravy stuck to a bowl.
I recite my alphabet, count to a hundred, do puzzles.
Mam squeezes my hand when the doctor says I'm lucky.
Not blind, not deaf or *worse.*

Later, I lie down naked
under enormous lights. I glow like an angel.
I want to spread my arms like wings
but I have to lie still. Hot.

On the way home I think about flying into space
in a spaceship full of bleeping machines and wires
or even just soaring past clouds on my angel wings.
The day is dark through the sunglasses I have to keep on.
The light hurts my eyes.

Mam tells me the sun-ray treatment will make me strong,
but I wear sunglasses all the time, even to watch telly.

For when I was a baby I had meningitis.

Distant Voices

Those Sunday mornings at the Mission,
the grip of socks around my ankles,
my taffeta skirt against the pew,
white-gloved hands genteely folded.
So many firm voices tear the moment
from a seamless bolt of days.

Let out, gloves and poses thrown aside,
hurtling through park to playground.
My brother's taunts, our mother's pleas
as we'd slide and spin
my eyes shut
against the always startling light.

Afternoons to Nana's, in her cramped room:
her clean pinny smoothed across her lap
ready for the tales to spill
from her children's children. Each one,
hair licked into place with spittle,
wanting nothing more
than Nana's glinting sixpence,
her approval pushed into our hands.

And then, play. A glance back:
the uncles talking smoke rings,
in that blue-hazed room, jokes,
their Sunday stout.
The aunts in the kitchen
making the best of Wonderloaf
and a slab of ripe cheddar, pickled cukes and onions.

Carried home through an otherworld
my head lolling against my father's shoulder
his jerky stride moving us
through the chequerboard night,
opened by quiet streetlamps in the dark
then closed, my eyes open, then closed.

Church Militant

Childhood Good Fridays
always darkened mid-afternoon
and Mum said *This is the moment*
He died, as she pulled the curtains closed.
And when I looked he was there, back-projected,
hanging limply, heaven's lowered shawl
draped over lifeless shoulders, and all around—
silence. All I wanted was to run
outside to play two-balls
on the kitchen wall.
To make the rhythm of the balls,
small thuds, sound like a reviving heart,
the pulse returning the blood, keeping it in
where it belonged. Giving life back to Jesus
for my mother, whose sadness
kept me curled in a chair
reading a book, escaping through
its traitorous, cheerful words.

Whit Walks (at Pentecost)

"In my sweet little Alice-blue gown
When I first wandered down into town
I was both proud and shy
As I felt ev'ry eye…"

Dressed in blue, flounces of lace
to the floor, I walk before the Whitsun queen,
scatter paper petals from the basket I carry.
Watch them flutter down like wings,
the Holy Spirit descending.

The band thumps out "Onward Christian Soldiers",
the queen, robed and flower-adorned, somehow
transplanted from the May, her subjects in procession
behind her. And I, pretty in Alice-blue, step royally,
smile for the cheering onlookers, think only
of the party at the Mission.

After the crowning of the queen, the hymns
and prayers— we get sandwiches
cut in triangles, shining ruby-red jelly,
solid blancmange.
The boys, collars and ties all askew,
chase the girls— a game of ticky-hit
round the back. I join in the fake screams,
my dress tucked into my knickers.

By half-past five, the queen has lost her crown,
(her mum and dad had been so proud). She leans
against the Mission wall, sucking long drags
on a plain Woodbine. Down the street, the faithful
are beckoned— the pub-door
swings open.

Break

I had a good home and I left
serves me jolly well right.

Arms linked reef-knot tight
Mum and I marched out
heels clacking in synch.
The walk from the bus home
shortened by our song against the wind
that slapped our faces, forced our voices louder
into giggles that tripped
over our mistakes.

Stand on a nick and you'll marry a brick
and a beetle will come to your wedding.

We avoided the nicks between paving stones
knowing our fate lay as much in those lines
as when we stretched our palms open
to the fortune teller at the fair.
We planted feet in adjacent squares
watched the ground,
kept within the prohibitions
neither of us trusting slabs of concrete
that would one of these nights
break, throwing us either side of a crevasse
too wide to join hands across.

Skies

Low, unrelenting grey, pressing down
on my childhood as I pumped myself
higher, higher, in Crowcroft Park,
the swing almost clearing the trees
and daisies shrinking then growing
as I went up in the air I could
never break through.
That sky wanted me down on the ground,
in my place, left to wonder what made clouds,
were they really angels' beds
and where was God?

Half-way round the earth and north,
the world with no top,
roof blown off, water sucked out into ice-floes,
leaving an open tract too focused on blazing blue
to bother with me, newly wondering:
here, nostril hair freezes at minus 25,
snow ploughs can carve a street back
from a barricade of drifts blown in overnight
and laden spruce branches bow down till snow slips
in a flurry that fills the air with a slow-motion,
blossoming, white mist.

A Northern Album

Purden Lake

" …music that will melt the stars."

If I had been dropped in here, into this small circular clearing, if it had been gouged out with no roads leading in, you'd never find me. I'd be alone at the base of a soundless dry well. I could walk, turn circles around the edges of gravelled earth but there would be no way out.

The only opening: up. Now, it's gaping black and deep, beginning to break out its intricate pattern of stars. If they were music, the stars would begin inaudibly, build slowly, gathering sound as more appeared. Is the music, are the stars constant, and only my attention lacking to perceive them? It takes a while but then I see the long trace, the shining blur that is the Milky Way: crescendo.

I know that some of these stars are dead. What I see is only light, millions of years away from the place where it started, light that long ago disappeared. Perhaps I can pull these from the sky. I could make some space in all that confusion of brightness. Find a way out. But what would I do with so much light? Could I hold it in my arms? Would it liquefy, run through my fingers and into the earth or remain hard-edged silver, prick my skin, what can light weigh?

The Artist's Wife

Wake to an empty space beside you
sheets undisturbed after the nights he spends
with another love, unable to leave
the sensuous lines on a smooth canvas skin.

Languish in the sharp-edged smell of turpentine,
linseed oil or damar varnish.
It hangs in the air for days
through all attempts to let it out:
windows and doors thrown open, or to smother it
with the scents of coffee brewing, muffins baking,
armfuls of roses carried into every room

It's a life of lies
as he tricks you into believing
three dimensions project from every flat surface.
He entices you along forest paths
to the edge of cliffs
and up into the vaulted ceilings of cathedrals.
You believe him. Then its gone
with one sweep of his brush.

But your eyes grow accustomed to noticing the sky
washed with the subtlest violet hue,
the monotone of a rock face splintered
into yellows, blues and greens

and when he does lie beside you he talks
through the screen of night,
the painted fabric of your life.

November Lights

Black and white dishes stack high
in a cold sink.

Walls loom grey
though I thought they were blue.
I slice vegetables. Mushrooms
pale into a shade of bone.
I can live without colour,
pare an onion sliver,
banish a tear.

November drips down the window,
the image blurs, becomes a fifties t.v.
out of tune. No theme song plays
as you arrive in the truck.
Move into focus.

Hero— in my kitchen—you proffer fire-flowers.
You must have scorched your hand
when you reached into the sun
for these dimpled circles of light.
Yellow, yellow. They bloom against sky-blue walls.

Hihium Colours

You are five thirty-nine, the dream-breaking,
the deep-shadowed winter
mornings, buzzer
bleating under your searching hand, pause,

head down, you lift
the darkness.

Once a year, late summer:
bright flashes light your face, crimsons, yellows,
strike the lake's surface as you cast
an Elk-Hair Caddis over
and over, let it rest a moment on the water.

Beside a river, you paint
the day in a rectangle of raw sienna,
thallo blue, mars violet. Colours
your eye takes from grass, sand,
water and sky.

You touch,
mark my body, pour moonsilver
on my breasts.

Hihium—Home

Because I remembered to return.
Because the bowl of the lake funnels the wind's harmony
to the loon's inexorable lament.
Because through this window are roughened trunks of pine,
wind-textured lake, hillside green and green and green.
Because distant spruce stand tall and thin,
straggly triangles, edges fuzzed.
Because the eagle zags its pale mark across this forest,
turns black against sky.
Because jack-pine branches reach low for the water's mirror.
Because whiskey jack flicks by the glass to the eaves,
chickadee falls like a pine-cone ready to scatter seed.
Because a full sky is stacked with clouds, flat-bottomed and luminous.
Because the kettle hums a promise on the wood-stove.
Because wind's vowels encircle our small night
as the moon looms, a silent, pellucid 'O'.

Captured

We climb from the lake, making
for the top of the ridge.
Plants want to touch us.
Ferns, uncurled,
risen fresh that day,
lick our legs to taste our intention.

Old man's beard drizzles against my face.
I brush away its tickle and tell you
this forest wants to have us, absorb us.

But you are already imagining the forest
captured, fixed in oils.
You look back and forward
as your fingers square a frame
for meagre twigs flicked from bare trunks,
and a path that slips its slim finger
through sprawling moss.

Another path that you will paint
into contemplation: softly scumbled
brushwork of trees, leaves, shadowed
undergrowth and patches of light
beckon, as if we might enter there and know
our destination.
For now, we push on,
uncertain of what lies ahead,
and, as the forest's silence clamours,
imagine we'll forget what we've left behind.

Genesis

When you go
you leave the radio on.
My arms and legs move
over the warmth of your shape.
My body sees you glowing infra-red.

The radio voice is a long way off
and I have followed
where space becomes time,
beyond all that is easily real, I'm drifting
across the blank black skies astronomers have photographed,
filtered back billions of light years
to images of galaxies forming,
nebulae twitching at the birth of stars.

The astronomers want the Beginning,
Sudden flash or slow eruption
that started Life.

Will they then deepen and lengthen exposures
to capture Before Life—another blank black expanse
or a drone, a buzz waiting to go off?

I want a photo of our space
not just before you left
when we lay here together
but right back to the start and beyond: before
this bed was made, before its tree was born,
when our love was out there, humming.

Traces

You are gone
from me, from our home.
Eager to claim my space, my time,
I gather up the bits you left behind. Shoes
eased off, one foot against the heel of the other
when you sat reading, too long, too late; your book
opened and turned face down; the mail
you had no time to open; on the balcony, your ashtray
piled high, dog-ends disintegrating in the rain (a rot
I stop my mind from contemplating).
Picking up, finding a place for things
tumbling from my overfull hands.

This is how my mother went round each room
after our visit, looking for books, toys,
jewellery we'd tossed aside then forgotten.
This is how mothers and fathers find
and hold onto the small, once insignificant,
treasures of a lost child; how bereaved
sons and daughters sift through
the layers of letters, cards, flowered and glittered
for every occasion, photos
that never made the albums, yellowed
recipes clipped years ago from the Woman's Page.
Death brings its demand for mementoes.

You are coming back,
sometimes I say, too soon. Let me keep
your books on the shelves,
your clothes in the drawers.
Good to be alone.
At night, I sit on the edge of our bed,
slip my arms into the sleeves
of your shirt, each small button's fastening
a painstaking measure of time.

The Comfort of Rain

In memory of Ann McQuaid

CIRCLE

I noticed emerald shoots of grass through moss,
memories pricking at the incantation
in my head, over and over: *Ann...maybe weeks,*
dying in slow motion.

A flicker in my eye, a brief sideways glance,
and the trees along the path jump toward me:
their smooth and naked lines, bars of a cell
move in, then open
on a Prince George spring.

> Cottonwood Island—
> gossamer seeds at river's edge,
> tufts of cottonwood-down,
> pompons in our hair.

> Away from the noise of neon along Central
> the seduction of used car lots,
> the pulp mill stench, we'd follow
> the Fraser, stand in Fort George Park
> as Aurora Borealis lit
> the city, its streets, stores and mills.

WOMAN'S TONGUE LEAF
(*Aspen, '81-'83*)

1.

Her smile welcomed
an extra pair of hands. Round and round
the table, picking up sheets of paper,
putting together *news*
by and for northern women.

Aspen leaves wag, shooting the breeze, she told me,
like women's tongues, women talking:
childcare, shiftwork, housework.
Pasting and printing done between day jobs
and night dreams: an end to violence, poverty.
Women's lives—always so much to say.

That spring, geraniums filled her window
full-blown and bold. I came afraid
of my thoughts, wore my black mood
like a hood. She made tea
and listened; her brilliant red flowers
patched the table with sunlight.

2.

Story-meetings: evenings at Paula's
for just one more of her squares.
Friday afternoons: wine bottle perched on the dresser,
cross-legged in Bronwyn's room—dolls and blocks
scattered, hands and knees, across the floor—kids!
Toys, books, sticky spots from honey spills, minding the children,
never-minding the rules. Laugh, cry, raise another beer—
never a glass, never "ladies", not us.

IMAGINE
(*April '83*)

Squares of red, yellow and blue
make a quilt of the park, spread,
ready for the picnic, sandwiches, muffins,
always zucchini bread and beer
surreptitious in coffee mugs, the final celebration.

The peace group built a cruise missile
in a garage, life-size—look, this is how small,
this is how it could sneak up on you
flash you into forever.
We made the Earth—papier-mache
over hooped sticks, look
how fragile.
Not her style, the idea to "die" on the streets;
talcumed-white skin, skeleton-suited
but, still, she lay down.
As generous as a nuclear bomb
we sprayed her ashen shape
to leave behind.

DEAR ANN

Any snow yet? Soon, I'm sure
for Hallowe'en. Fairies and goblins all
fattened with woollies and here,
Little Red Devils, their spirits dampened.

She stayed. I went
south in search of February's
sudden optimism: purple, yellow,
white crocus-spikes and the comfort
of rain.

Our children grew between the lines
of our letters, five hundred
miles apart, we dissented
at school meetings, cheered at soccer.

Visits came less
than cards & words
under dazzling
"Starblanket & Fires."
                    We're all a bit older.

In silhouette

I'm scanning the sky
and the high branches of silhouetted trees
for an eagle to break through
this resolutely, chalk-grey morning,
raise a little drama as it swoops and settles in
against a sheltering trunk, its hunched posture
ornamental and only an occasional twitch of its head
to belie its carved indifference, its quick eye
ready to detect a tremble, a rustle in the scrub,
its wings will lift air in a maelstrom of movement,
a swift descent to snatch a morning's meal

There is no eagle, nor a mouse
to dash into the open. Nothing
can move pinned against this sky.
No suggestion of a break, no cloud
that might shape itself,
detach, let sunlight press
a halo at its edges.
Only the ragged remains of a crow's nest
lodged in a tree but coming apart
like a ball the neighbourhood kids have kicked
to shreds then booted up there and abandoned.

Walking here, after I learned she was dying,
I promised to always look for the openings
between the trees. My thoughts stay shut
like heavy black curtains
pulled across a stage, the theatre closed for the season.
Surely, if I wait in the gloom, the music will rise.

Farewell

On the way in to the lake
the washboard road
rattles us, loosens the joints.
Edges blur. Wilderness, bright patches of colour
against shadow,
translucent lake and sky.
Beside the road an oddly shaped rock,
dark and out of place, shape-shifts into bear
and a moose cow and calf stand, the mother
lifts her head slowly as we pass.

We arrive to cowboy coffee from an enamelled pot
sipped through a skim of grounds.
We troll all day, hope trout will nibble
our willow-leaf spiral, wedding-band lure.
Wed to this lake! They can't resist.

The round and perfect ululation of a loon
in mourning; the sky, basin of trees, lake
and we are stilled, at its centre.
The fish, hooked through one eye
is undersized, cast back.
A bald eagle swoops,
breaks open the lake's surface, snatches the fish,
lifts, turns
its silver head
to the moon.

We shake the pan
and huddle round the fire
that shouts our presence into
the pervading black, sparks
flying up, our eyes drawn to the sky's stories.

We crack another beer,
drink to the lake that never fails.

What We Keep

Beside an Ocean, Under a Sky

This is not all there is
about this place. The quiet,
brushed through grass,
thin feathered stalks
and strong stems
that resist the wind,
ragged-edged dock and vetch,
its purple hoods in showy bloom;
the rapid dip and rise of a swallow,
the interruption of its trill.
In the distance, a flock of gulls
lifts like a sun-bleached net
shaken out then settled down.

Plants scramble for growth
before land gives way
to sand stretched to the sea.
Across flat, brown wetland: logs
left by the tide, shining swipes of water
and, far off, pylons stand, unsteady
reminders of the old oyster-shucking pier.

And we've slipped ourselves in here
on this rare afternoon of our own.
You balance your easel
on the rocks. I stumble down,
set my chair.
Each of us pursuing a version of colour and tone,
not knowing what will pull the eye or heart,
close and apart, as lovers
must always be.

You will see the shapes of things,
sketch an outline, arrange colour and form
the way you place argument.
And I will move round and round,
my words escaping from me
until I gather them in
like unruly children, line them up
across a blank page.

This afternoon we do not speak.
Later, I climb back to you,
look over your shoulder,
find that in our silent, separate way
we have each arrived
at the vast, lilac-washed and vibrant sky.

Nitobe—Reflections

Japanese Maples, their colours thinning,
lean toward water.
Exposed branches, bowing,
they present their leaves to earth.
The lawn slopes to the pond's edge.

Leaves scatter
the pond's deep green, its obscure darkness;
lie on the surface like the piping of a flute
breaking over the basso profundo.
The whole tree reflected, slow music
seeping up from beneath the water.

Nitobe—Water Lily

In this garden of undulations
I want to smoothe the curve of lawn
the way I move my hand over the rise of your hip

and listen to trees, breathe
reflections into the pond, to surface
like shot silk.

At the silent end of a long summer day
I wish to wax high on the arch of this bridge,
let night come down
on my pale body
afloat, a water lily, opened
under a naked moon.

Reflection

First night in this house above the ocean,
glass is revealing its nature—liquid,
pulsing black, wind stirring the surface
of the window, waves lifted
from a brimming sea.

Below us ghosts leap from the water,
moon white
into fluid night.

Night is close against the window.
The clock, three framed photos
and our faces reflect from the wind-shaken dark.
The wall in the glass shivers.
Your arm, reaching behind my shoulders
may or may not touch me.

You touch me and I turn to you,
an easy moment that doesn't know
our bodies have held us apart.
Nothing's the same
after a storm.
Driftwood shifts, dunes change shape,
plants are uprooted and blow away.
Skeins of seaweed lie across a gutted beach.

Morning, calm. A parasailer
waits on the headland
to take to the silk. He'll glide
on the updrafts, know the sky as bird
then land—on his feet,
gather the blue and purple sail in his arms,
feel its sudden weight.

Ocean in a Room

Low tides, we lay on the rock, believing it alive,
burning ourselves against its body heat,
sure of blood pulsing under its pock-marked skin,
lichen curled as pubic hair.

You slipped into the clear depth of water, went under
to find how far down the blue could go; found anemones,
sea-stars, darting fish eager for shadows;
broke surface, offered me an oyster on your palm.

Now, I have your canvas. The tide is in, rock submerged,
softened by drizzled light caught on the curve of each small wave.
Ocean at rest in my living room, its surface
dipped by a slack tide, stretches back to a comfortless shore.

The water still so blue, the rock, washed in the colours of your palette
is smaller than I remember, and cold.

Temperate

Last summer: one elongated cloud
stretched low, the length of Slocan Lake, as if
it had been piped in, white icing-edge
stolen from a wedding cake. A clear
morning all around it, above, dense
purple template of mountain, below, tension
of the lake holding back the certainty
that fish will rise.

And here again: cloud-line cuts across
the Coast Mountains this early
morning, peaks lifted beyond
my contemplation.
Landscape proferred
in layers, as if the whole
would be a revelation,
too huge, would call down a deluge
and I would drown.

Silent Film

Out my window, rain
cuts straight lines down
a lingering shot of a cottonwood
in new-leafed disarray, a tired cedar,
one telephone pole and a streetlight.

It's movie rain. The kind that drenches
lovers as they clutch and kiss,
ignore water channelling down their necks.
Silk clothes cling.
Passion steams.

My picture is a mood piece. No people.
The cottonwood has a loose branch.
It sways, caught at one end. I wait.

I dial six numbers, get five disembodied voices
that are sorry they can't speak to me. One
real person cuts in— can she call me back
later? Just dashing out.

It rains. The branch hangs.

Always, Two Voices

At the centre of this lake we drift
in a small boat. From the stern, you watch the surface
for the flick and shimmer of sudden small wings,
Trout already glinting in your imagination,
you tell me the flies on the lines are a match
for the ones that are hatching.
I sit with my back to the bow and watch.

The burnished coin of the sun
slips behind the ridge and silence drops.
Everything is evening as light transfers
sky to lake, pink and pale blue
striations across the water, deepening
to lavender as a cloud passes
and your fishing line pulls its reflection behind us.
The lake seals itself hard and smooth,
and everything is held,
until the boat glides into tree-shadows
toward the black uncertain edge.

A shudder ripples the water.
You reel in quick and steady, but the trout's too small.
As you set it free the loons wail a single round note
that falls to a sob and in reply the frogs,
at the other end of the lake, are working
into a frenzy, layer upon layer of insistent syllables.

You turn back. I ache for warmth.
As we head for shore I am thinking
of how, soon, you'll be out there alone.
In the dark, the boat will shine silver
and slide, as if the loon's cry is an invisible thread,
pulling; the frogs' distracting clatter,
another demand to be heard.

And I will sit on the porch of our cabin,
holding to me the comfort of tea,
of keeping my watch.

What Enters

The tide is in now.
I take its easy susurrus into my mouth,
find the flow and fall of its soft, percussive drag.

What's left behind as water retreats:
scattered and broken shells, sprinklings
of minute winkles and barnacled rocks
as unbreachable as mountains.

Breath enters the way mist slides
over the warm earth at dawn. It curls and sidles, hides
beneath the surface of skin: stirrings
of wings pushing into first light,
fissures in a black sky
silver-edged and glinting, gashes in silk.

When I breathe
this way there is nothing beyond the in,
then out.

Ocean Bed

(for Lilian)

I curl into my mother
whose hair flows, long
undulations of a silvered ocean.
We of water, lie in it silent
as a drift of seaweed, buoyant,
as pale and delicate as sponges.

Sunlight infuses and warms us.
I press my spine into the pillow of her, *spooning*
we used to say when I was three
and climbed into her high, soft-as-flesh bed
with its mounds of sheets, blankets
and quilt—a stilled night sea patched
by moonlight.

We lie together, ourselves
sweet-smelling waters,
her womb turned inside out
and both of us home.

Some Days

I come here to cry.

Along the lower trail that leads to the pond,
plants push through a chaos of growth
fed by the moist and richly-rotted soil along the creek.
This is where I learned to forage for chamomile,
a friend showing me how it persists all winter
in ragged patches beneath tough grasses,
their coarse blades bent to the rain.

Where the path rises and bends, broad trunks
of cottonwoods are spaced between alders,
make a silent room, their branches spread
to make a ceiling, a space apart
from judgment where I can listen
to the resounding toll of endings.

Three times this week, news of illness, deaths
of friends—too young—
stirs memories of those already gone. Walk and walk,
tread into earth the plants that thrive
over mounds that cover tonnes of garbage. This park
was once the city dump. So much we have thrown
away, discarded and chosen to forget except,
here and there, a flute of steam rises,
thin whiff of what lies hidden.

I make this place my retreat,
shut-down, so little light
seeping through this January morning.
There will be no imaginings of a new day's new blooms,
light caught within them and held, an hour,
a week, a season. This morning,
I will allow no stirrings
of change to ring the pure bell
that signals all beginnings.

What We Keep

Going back is like a foreign trip,
we speak the language as if it's home,
wake eager for each day,
certain of sun, the shade of forests.
We dip our toes, rivers
surge and stay in one spot,
right there, for us. Nothing
moves on.

Wine and cheese and bread
from a basket, but we won't speak of the journey—
losing the luggage, nearly missing the train,
whose child threw up before we'd started,
the days it rained.

No, don't take my picture!
Let me straighten my hair, wipe away the tears,
smile for the camera—
a keeper for the album.

Eevy, Ivy, Over

Bluebells, cockle shells, eevy, ivy, over.

In the school-yard, starched white pinafores
over patched and pocketed hand-me-downs,
ruffle and shift, purple stretch-leggings,
flashing neon runners, bounce.
Annie and the girls, my Rosa and her friends
I'm watching you all
as the rope turns bigger arcs, Annie takes a run,
in — Rosa pulls her legs up, well off the ground,
will they fix in mid-air?
Stay two seconds for the rope to slice
into Annie's time, flip the girls
into inspection lines as Miss comes
ringing her bell.

> Each lass made herself smart,
> lips locked and stiff arms out
> for the ruler's put-away tap or the smack
> of the order, "Get inside and scrub them!"
> Annie was good at the morning head-work,
> regiments of curling letters that never
> broke apart, never leapt from their line
> into a word or to whisper a sound.
> Afternoons, lasses learned to be wives:
> tight rows of stitches hemmed a bit of calico
> or joined two scraps, a seam and fell.
> Annie learned the catch and pull of a needle,
> nodded *yes Miss*, but she bade her time
> for the break she'd make,
> fingers crooked and grabbing the stuff of her skirts
> as she'd run out the Girl's End, past the tin-plate factory,
> a rhythm in its racket calling for her.

And Rosa, on our walk home from school,
ignores my calls, makes off down the hill:
fistfuls of blossoming blue skirts
pulled up to her thighs, runs, hair flying,
lands flat-footed in the wet, the murk of a black puddle,
delicious mud streaking her boots, her legs, and
she laughs, laughs in never-ending, spiralling echoes.

Into the Light

She learned autumn had turned to winter that night
in December when we stood, our boots squelching in mud
as we shifted our feet and placed them down,
searching out firmer ground, and as we did
we also let our bodies sway, a tentative dance
to the music of drums, saxophones and bells,
an odd but joyful orchestra that told us to banish the dark,
lift our lanterns up to the sky. Candles and tea-lights
inside houses of glowing tissue and rice-paper,
cans punched through with holes like stars, like moons
or the sun.

It was the sun we were after.
That damp and clouded night that earlier
had offered us nothing but the return of rain,
was now bright with hundreds of small suns
drifting in front of faces lifted to the promise of light
and the huge-spoked and fiery circle on the top of the mound
burned, its flames eating the dark.
In the solstice fire, I told her, burns our wish for the sun
to return, knowing how she would wake
each morning, wanting winter to bring snow.

It has come at last. Snow that quietly fills the gaps
in the world: woodland spaces between trees and scrub,
between the branches of the trees, sprawling
space along the streets, between parked cars
and newspaper vending boxes and down into corners
where walls meet, filling and filling
and changing everything.
And now, for her, snow is forever. The hill
is a playground where she tumbles and slides,
a puffed-up, lolloping snow creature that talks
to the snowmen guards at the soft edges of this room
that, like laughter, is big and true but will quickly
fall apart and melt away.

As we stumble home and she kicks at snow past her knees,
I hear through the empty whiteness of the afternoon,
thin but strong, the mirrored notes of two chickadees
looking for spring.

The Promise

The bird I've never seen has returned
to trees too tall and too many.
Even in bare February there's no shape
to match the coral sound of its piping.

Its disembodied song comes to tell me
that songbirds exist
though winter has denied them
and I have forgotten.
They descend into uncertain days
as sun gathers strength to lighten air,
disperse grey, open sky into its true colour.

The robin is brash enough to perch close by,
no secrets in its shrilling
that declares my backyard taken.
The hidden bird's song
is as loud
but less assured. Two notes,
not a question but tentative. Listen:
soon-soon, soon-soon.

This I hold, and its promise.
Enough.

Harbinger

Change cracks through
February's shell, sun re-shapes
laurel leaves outside my window.
This robin is the new season's messenger
warbling thrush-like to my foreign ear.

Robin of that other time
was small and round
plumped against an easterly blow,
perched on snow, Christmas cards.

That time was when we were immortal,
pain was a dentist; loss was a glove,
an umbrella on a bus.
This time I'll open up the present wider,
make space for the future
to climb in.

Correspondence

Only connect

A February night on the beach, we stumble
toward water's edge, the sky clouded. We look to the city,
 its smug brightness, then back to the bay
its small, hopeful points of illumination, boats and buoys.
Harbour lights flash red and white. Reflections
are multi-coloured skeins proffering a deceptive path
from here to there, where buildings' lit and unlit rooms
are checkered against the certain black of the mountains.

Such a narrow strip of life, and then the quiet dark.

Quiet all around this island night.
Dark all around our silence, until
far down the beach, a soft-edged light begins
to turn. A pattern, a rhythm burns, and we realise
torches spin in invisible hands and together we watch
their semaphore of connection flame in circles of fire.

Acknowledgements

My thanks to those people who, over the years this book has been growing, have read and provided invaluable feedback on the poems and encouraged me: Eileen Kernaghan, Sue Nevill and Clelie Rich, the members of the Sage Hill Poetry Colloquium, Don McKay, Patricia Young, Lorna Crozier, Roo Borson and Stephanie Bolster. I could not forget the inspirational group of poets I worked with in the advanced poetry seminar in the Creative Writing Department at the University of British Columbia, Jennica Harper, Fiona Lam, Laisha Rosnau, Jennifer Scott, and particularly George McWhirter whose advice was spoken in poetry itself.

I would like to thank the editors of the periodicals and publications in which some of these poems, sometimes in different versions, have been previously published: *The Amethyst Review, The Antigonish Review, Contemporary Verse 2, Dandelion, Descant, Event, Grain, Museletters, The New Orphic Review, The New Quarterly, Orbis* (UK), the anthology *Letting Go* (Black Moss, 2005), the chapbook anthology *Love in Four Positions* (Leaf Press, 2003), the web-site of Leaf Press and the collection, *Quintet: Themes and Variations* (Ekstasis Editions, 1998).

My thanks for the germ of the idea of a young woman who wanted to know "how will it get out" in "The Local Woman Who 'Did'", to Elizabeth Roberts and her excellent oral history of working class women, *A Woman's Place*. The epigraph to "Whit Walks" is from the song lyrics of Alice Blue Gown by McCarthy and Tierney, 1919. For details of school routines and rules for girls in the poem "Eevy, Ivy, Over" I turned to Barry Turner's *Equality for Some: the Story of Girls' Education*. Quotes in italics in the poem "Break" and in the epigraph to "Eevy, Ivy, Over" are from traditional folk rhymes. The epigraph to "Purden Lake" is from Gustave Flaubert's *Madame Bovary,* translated by F. Steegmuller. The title *Imagine* is from the song by Lennon and McCartney. The quote in "Dear Ann" is after an image by Alice Olsen Williams, depicted on a greeting card. And, lastly, "Only Connect" is from *Howard's End* by E.M. Forster.

Sincere and special thanks to my dear friend Jean Mallinson whose skillful editorial guidance is always offered and gratefully received and to Stewart, Thomas and Rosa for their love and patient support.